My mother agrees with the dead

My mother agrees with the dead

Joan and all her beautiful poems! xx Susan

SUSAN STENSON

Susan Stenson

©Susan Stenson, 2007

No part of this publication may be reproduced, stored in a retrieval system or transmitted, in any form or by any means, without the prior written consent of the publisher or a licence from The Canadian Copyright Licensing Agency (Access Copyright). For an Access Copyright licence, visit www.accesscopyright.ca or call toll free to 1-800-893-5777.

Cover photograph: istock.com
Cover design: Rachel Rosen
Author's photograph: Billie Stenson
Typeset in Bernhard Modern
Printed in Canada by The Coach House Printing Co,
Toronto, Canada

The publishers gratefully acknowledge the support of the Canada Council for the Arts, the Ontario Arts Council and the Book Publishing Industry Development Program (BPIDP) for their financial assistance.

Wolsak and Wynn Publishers Ltd
69 Hughson Street North, Suite 102
Hamilton, ON
Canada L8R 1G5

National Library of Canada Cataloguing in Publication Data

Stenson, Susan,
    My mother agrees with the dead / Susan Stenson
Poems.
ISBN 978-1-894987-18-9

1. Grief--Poetry.   2. Compassion--Poetry.   I. Title.
PS8587.T365M9 2007   C811'.54   C2007-900304-4

For Rosemary

CONTENTS

One

The little mother knows	13
Snow	15
At the airport	16
Make believe	17
Late October	18
Greek urn	19
Propped up by a sunny window	20
Brazen, young	21
Death can't help Jim build the fence	22
Love poem	23
The fumbling of things	24
Card game	25
Our Lady of Mercy	26
Dinner party	27

Two

Tell me, tell everyone	31
Those spiders in a jar	32
Saturday nights	33
Widow's song	34
Ask for birds	37
Heirlooms	38
Wake	39
Nothing special	40
Rain	41

Three

Big sky	45
Sylvan Glen	46
Bedside	47
Hide the pies	48
The myriad sympathies	49
Taxidermist	50
Lullaby	51
Still life	52
Grief in the world	53
Stroke	54
Her breathing, for example	55

Four

Praise for humans	59
Air travel	60
Stones	61
Ground	62
The shallow pool	63
Wooden chair	64
Details	65
The cormorant	66
Making jam	67
Humbly	68
Hope	69
Crazy maps	70
Acknowledgements	71

ONE

THE LITTLE MOTHER KNOWS

1.

Everybody's poor so it doesn't matter. One skirt, two sweaters.
But she drops out of school anyway to work at the Bata Shoe
and makes good money. Turns it all in at home.
They never tell her anything. She thinks she cut herself on a rock,
that day in August, swimming alone at the end of the pier,
never imagines what becoming a woman means
and never thinks to ask. She's not afraid of her father,
a man who can't stand a fly in the house after the war,
a man must forget the bunkered world, the beauty
in his daughter's face too much to look at sober.
Evelyn, he calls for his wife, *get the swatter, kill it quick.*

2.

Don't those Baltimore tramps have a home?
Her father likes to make himself the fool.
Can't meet anyone. Can't go anywhere.
He is the Catholic but never makes it up the hill to mass.
She's the one who wants to become a nun.
Loves to sing. But the priest changed that.
Father Parry, the old fool, thinks she was born yesterday.
She races down Pine Street, over the tracks, home.
Never knows how pretty she is. Those sweet muscles,
legs. Rags to curl her hair with. Lets Ada dress her.

3.

She lives the way she dies: in a hurry,
because everybody wants a piece of her.
Even shares her mother's womb with brother Ron.
Always find something for the collection plate.
If there is no money in a purse before payday,
it means she can't spend it. Curl up on the couch
with a good book and listen to the wind. Amen.
Love your kids. Don't spoil them at Christmas.
She washes floors on her knees. Never owns a mop.
Don't make your face worse than it is.
She can't believe she said that. You know what she means.
If a man steals, that's dirty.
If he cheats at cards, he's never coming home.
Refuses to dance on a Saturday? He'll never marry.
Don't fool yourself.

4.

She never says the F word. Works on the line
in the packing room at Nicholson File so hears
it all. Can't believe how some women talk.
The young ones can't keep up with her though
but she hates the games they play with the foreman:
what they call him behind his back, embarrassed
to repeat it, but frankly, that's exactly how she feels.
Can't bear the heat, especially the afternoons
in July when the sun sneaks in off the lake, the
last few hours, doesn't know how she makes it through.
It raises her kids. She's not complaining.
Needs five minutes peace when the house is quiet,
time for a crossword or fold the last load.
Two weeks holiday, same time each summer: takes the kids
to the zoo. Stops at the Chinaman's for coke on the way home.
Don't ask for anything in here. Keeps the straws.

5.

Never walks, always runs.
She can throw a ball from centre, home.
Why would God make children go hungry?
She'll have a thing or two to say about that.
Won't travel to funny countries.
Lives and dies in the town where she is born.
Never understands the other side of the world.
Can't give things away fast enough.
Her mother's door, too, marked with an X,
the hobo sign for charity rubbed on the sidewalk.

6.

Never make kids afraid of thunder.
Mother knows the world is crooked and there's nothing
she can do about that but it doesn't mean she's playing along.
Can't tell you how many men come looking.
Luckily, she can go without. Some women need sex,
but she walks up town to pay her bills. Breaks her collarbone
when she falls out of the tree. With seven brothers, she learns
to run, won't put up with that horseshit. Weighs
the same as she did on her wedding day.
One thing she can't do: choose a coffin. Figures
God is as practical as she is so she never prayed
for anything she couldn't use. When she dies,
there's not one sock or shoe she hasn't worn.

SNOW

It starts like the credits before a film begins,
everything noted and itemized to draw you in
to some semblance of order, expectation, routine,
a this-too-shall-pass reverie. While some go
for popcorn, napkins, wine,
you stay glued to the screen.

Or it starts with a sore stomach,
a little gas, a slight light-headedness:
overreacting to spicy food or too much
caffeine but the doctor shakes her head
and calls for tests at the lab
while you discuss the weather and the colour
the receptionist is wearing and the line-ups everywhere
but never ever will you think of saying,
What do you think we can do about this?

Or loathe to sleep alone, reluctant
in the apartment after dark
although you've lived by yourself for twenty years.
Things change. Wouldn't you know.

Inevitably, there are urologists.

And soon enough, oncologists and nurses
who come to the house and drink your coffee,
then ask, *Do you know the man across the street?*
(where she will be going next) but you don't.
She drains the mug, sets it down beside the sink.

Your car, Friday, gives up on the way to the hospital,
accelerator keels over only a mile from town, then
the car pulls to the side like it knows the spot.

You take your time finding the flashing lights,
notice you're wearing your slippers
and they make you laugh, those slippers,
the car at the side of the road, someone
calling your name in a room full of people
and no one answering, no one hearing it, really.

At the airport

These days it's a household word, somebody
new to welcome home, pull up a chair,
scramble the eggs, chemo on Thursday,
morphine beside the butter next to the coffee.
A dog in the corner hasn't been walked
for days, yawns from the deeper part of the craw.
We accept mortality, right? The dog
moves in with the young ones next door.

At the airport, I tell you about my mother.
You tell me about your son. I can't eat.
We sit sipping tea in the cafeteria,
a Monday afternoon, returning
from hospital visits to jobs in the city.
You order the Kelowna Special,
eventually, I follow, pepper steak,
and fries, for once, instead of salad.

Back home, I pick apples off the tree
in the yard, like everyone does
at this time of year, place the small ones
on the sill to sun, wait for the prognosis,
thick brown apple sauce to slather
on chunks of rye bread, catch myself
crossing fingers under the breakfast nook,
spot a squirrel and a sparrow on the feeder.

Make believe

September. A doctor tells my mother to get her things
in order and if it could, all hell would really break loose
trying to get a handle on what it is he means exactly.

Policies, painkillers, lawyers, long-distance calls,
and *What do they charge these days to light a candle
at St. Anthony's across town?*

She's never been sick a day in her life.
And what doctor can explain it?
This one doesn't take much time.

Anyway, to see an oncologist will take months, one, two, three?
She'll be dead by then but Mother doesn't seem to mind.
Get your things in order, the doc repeats, *Get your things . . .*

Nothing makes me believe this is happening.
But since the news I call every day. Discuss the weather
like I'm dating a meteorologist: *just a sec'* while he resets the barometers.

October. We've both stopped drinking. We make lists.
Call the lawyer, check the will. Book the hall. Buy the coffin.
Clean the fridge. Visit Edna. Fix the zipper on the silk blouse.

LATE OCTOBER

Mother copies pages from her Bible.
Having lost her glasses, her nose touches
the table like a child pulling each
stroke of the pencil from line to line,
as if it's important to get it right. She
finishes, takes my hand, leads me to
the top of the stairs to coat, hat, cane
but we can't find her shoes.

In Japan, they tell me to prepare for death
with poems. Important to say the piece
in front of loved ones, to speak
what has never been spoken, the breath
inside of words, so many poems
to describe death in Japan, the word's
a small phrase: *death in war, death
in accident, death in hospital bed.*

Mother and I make it to the hall.
As far as we walk today, the top
of the stairs, both of us dressed
for a cold day on the town,
but we don't move. How to say goodbye?
*Death with crossword open on the table?
Death in late October? Death in daughter's arms.*

GREEK URN

Mother put my name on the white vase
that sits (has always sat) on the wooden table
(that used to belong to Aunty Phil)
on the landing at the top of the stairs.

Putting my name on it means I get it
when she dies. *Put your name on it*
she yells from the kitchen,
if you don't hurry, someone else will.

All night I cut tape into tags.
Upend the junk drawer, want
the plastic corn-on-the-cob forks
and Jersey cow magnet. Pick the
platter and a wide-mouthed jar.
Mother stays awake with *Crossword City*,
obsessed with filling in the squares.

I don't need any of this stuff,
home is 3000 miles from here.
What's a five letter word
for Greek urn? she yells
without looking up. She uses a pen
and makes a mess of things.
A Greek urn? Can't we just call the Sally Ann?

For once she's silent.
I'll have to make it up to her.
What will I do with all these shoes?
The bowling trophies, the children's Bible?
There are photos stuffed in Bata Shoe bags
under the bed. (She wants to know
what else is under there.)
You tell her. I can't look.

PROPPED UP BY A SUNNY WINDOW

She dies just five months after painting
our kitchen, seventy-four and not yet frail.

We watch life shrink to good and bad
days: hours, minutes, seconds, breaths.

No wheelchairs. No nudge. No fevers. No nod.
No strange conversations beside the bed, either,

in rooms filled with women strapped to chairs,
propped up by a sunny window – why

it seems so impossible this goodbye,
not children now among the dead.

The whole town stands in the cold. At the funeral
Father John shakes each hand, does not squeeze,

a certain touch is necessary when it rains.
The kind of day we'll remember in our bones.

BRAZEN, YOUNG

I see them at the far table in the St. Lawrence Hotel.
I'm at the bar. Let my eyes adjust to the dim light.
Father cups a 10 cent draft in one hand, cigarette in the other.

Mother looks smart. Her coat, almost paid for, cashmere.
It's Saturday — take it slow. Nothing happens here
Nothing much. It's the future they're waiting for.

Father shaves twice a day. Change shoved deep in the pockets.
The war has followed them. They order another round.
Across the room, Jimmy Hart sells cigars, wheelchair

against the wall: Something they will try to teach me
but I'll never get it right. Steal coal. Drink whisky.
Kiss the girl: the inevitable growing up. She's Catholic

and almost thirty. He's not. Tonight, the stars have loose tongues.
I join them for last call. Discuss wedding plans.
What would they like to know? I ask them, brazen, young,

bold: a fortune teller brushing the curls of the queen.
I have said too much. The whole room stops now.
Mother finishes her drink, keeps the eyes low.

I'm not afraid of you, she says. Stands up.
Puts her arm into the left sleeve, the right.
Leaves a tip on the table under the glass.

DEATH CAN'T HELP JIM BUILD THE FENCE

We found Granny sitting straight up
in the claw-foot, chest deep, water
still warm. Who doesn't want to die
like that? Like plugging in the kettle,
like peeling an orange in one long strip.

Because dying can be all thumbs,
making a mess of things trying
to be gentle: treatments Tuesdays,
this pill, that pill, time-released pain killers
and their flat-on-your-back implications,
their down-on-your-knees-saying-please delegations.

I'll say it first: We're not afraid,
Death, but move out of the kitchen.
There's no room in Harry's garden
either, so don't be putting on your
gumboots or the straw hat
you tried on at the market
last weekend. Put down that rake.

Everybody's waiting and Jim's needing
help building the fence – what can you do?
Measure? Saw? Your skills are few, Death –
fetch the beer, the level, then what?

LOVE POEM

I'll be there. Stop fussing. Get your wet thumb away from that
cow-lick you call bangs. Kleenex, spat on, is not face cloth.
That's dimple, not mayo, chocolate, not beauty mark. I said
I'd be there. I could change my mind! Leave you bent over the
toilet, retching from the nausea of the cure we all ran for last
week, planting our pink ribbons breast-high, hooked to the
sport bra, the spandex, the headband, the perspiration (not
sweat) accumulating on our sun-kissed foreheads: retching in
the middle of the night. Sleep another thing to get through.
I'll be there when you give up talking. It will only be the eyes
now, I'm guessing, that will speak. Whisper, wheeze, the ooze
and flattery blinking shut longer than blinking open and with
your little head on the pillow, too, breath's a simple rise in
the field of your chest. For pity. I can't watch. All those giddy,
inoperable years where every word from your mouth stung the
smallest parts of me. Clitoris, ulna, wrist, the colours around
a cut, tremolos of purple, yellow, orange, red, a small mole
called brown.

THE FUMBLING OF THINGS

The nights scratch and whisper, everything
I've tried to put into words leans against the dark.
Tonight is quiet but I can still hear water
in the pipes, the newborn's cough, then cry
and just as startling, his return to sleep.

Hear my sister home from her long shift.
Home from rooms where windows and the ill
keep covered up. Were there fewer artifacts,
I would call these rooms empty, square,
suitable, without the fumbling of things.

No TV guides, no spilled mints,
no dice or fuzzy slippers. Space
has no concern with the future:
a chair, a stool, beige curtains.
Rooms so much kinder to the dead.

CARD GAME

It's a bad hand, two
nines and no trump
for a man recovering
from surgery, snaps
the deck, throws it flat
and tells his wife to *kiss ass*,
for no apparent reason.

A phrase I'm told
is a job site hazard
hard on the hats
of men's tongues.

The wife
silent like the words
fly off his lips at regular intervals
and how might she get even?

We are witnesses.
We will testify at the funeral:
Yes, we will say, *it was slow*
and yes, we will say, *it was mean.*

Husband limps to the bathroom,
while Wife whispers *tests aren't so good.*
Next week another specialist
in a fancy office to dispense
a future none of us will repeat.

We play cards and focus on the rules.
There must be something we can do.
Careful not to trump a partner's ace,
we count and stack the deck
as if our lives depend upon it.

Drive home the way we know.
No moon, high beams.

OUR LADY OF MERCY

She knows Rose has passed on
but doesn't iron the blouse, or dig out
the skirt from the back of the closet.
She wipes one good shoe and stops
– can't say how she's arrived: This house
at the top of the hill across the street
from the Catholic church where last year she
buried the brother, buried the parents and now
the sister – where she goes once a week
and sits at the back, where the light
shines clear and thin on the pew.

At Rose's funeral, Margaret can't tell you
how she knows nothing's settled, not this house,
not this town, not anybody looking. She sees
her nephew reeling close to the grave, his first
funeral, but Margaret, more experienced,
stands further back, leans against a tree,
lights a cigarette but it's useless in the wind.

Margaret's not sure where she's going
when she pulls out of the cemetery following
the long line of cars heading to the Legion Hall
so it doesn't matter if she turns left instead of right
at the top of town or if she stops at the little place
by the bridge, when it starts to rain, she pulls over.

She's not tired by her grief, that's not what she would say
if it came up in conversation. Margaret would not tell you,
for example, that the lake at this time of year looks like one
apologetic yawn but if you saw her looking, saw her standing now
at river's edge where it changes from narrow to wide
near the viaduct, you might think you know exactly
what she sees.

26

DINNER PARTY

It's your turn to entertain the guests
tonight. They'll all show up: the twins,
the girls, the lame, the clumsy,
Eve and Rhea, Red and Bim. But
I know, you're tired of being kind.

It's time to prepare the meal,
watery peas for Emma (she died
in the convalescent home). Uncle Jacob
(throat cancer at the Jubilee), takes extra
pepper in the soup until it sings.

Pick fresh greens from the garden for
Billy (drowned in Port Hope harbour)
likes a splash of vinegar on the spinach
after a three-minute steaming so be sure
to strain that bit of water from the pan.

There are not enough chairs
and still the dead keep coming.
Conversation's never easy. Keep it light.
Try speaking of the husbands, the children.
Mention the lonesome, the homely, the kind.

Wearing their cardigan sweaters, they
expect the best and you to serve the drinks:
Emma whistles better now that she's dead,
martini, no olives, wet.

TWO

TELL ME, TELL EVERYONE
for Brian

You wear that scarf for your father
who died last winter because you can't
believe anyone loves like this: slow,
diurnal scribbling in a thin journal with
penciled serif. Each day, a diary recording

your mother's outfits, the hose, the tweed,
the silk blouse, the pearl earrings.
Couldn't embarrass her by forgetting
what she had worn the day before. A man
like that. A story you tell me, tell everyone.

Your mother lives in a home, cannot say
what has brought you to her side today.
She's just a woman waiting for the rest
of her life, a Sunday drive, maybe, jam.
And you, these days, only good for so much.

Walk the hurried hills behind the house
like a man repeating what he must remember:
love has nothing to do with the heart. Walk
carefully on these stones, Brian, between
the rain flowers, the baboon blossoms,
aloe's bright petals such weary messengers
in this humble light prostrate at your feet.

THOSE SPIDERS IN A JAR

Nobody's allowed to get real close because
a boy's just a kid in a small town. But the
bird – dropped by the mysteries outside
the kitchen window – is ours, so hands off.

We stare like we do at Sunday school:
too many elbows and not enough bench,
bow-tied and bored – Yes, it's dead – so
something's gotta' be done. March like

mini-pallbearers, solemn, sure-footed
down the lane to the lake. Want to hold it.
Want to see what the fuss is all about:
spiders in a jar, mosquito, moth, frog.

Last winter, Leo's dog. Then Mr.
Skibinski, then Gran. Take turns
passing bird from boy to boy to box
turned coffin in the centre of the dock:

marbles, string, paperclips, rock,
everything we've got falls into that box,
so the bird can return, comfortable now
with whatever it is that's down here.

SATURDAY NIGHTS

When they climb the hill, their mouths open wide
to the hoot and the history of moon, teenagers
drinking canned beer and howling, after dark,

when faith unpacks the voices stumbling
over the highest Douglas Fir, then – crashing
through my living room windows.

Sometimes they can't find their way, miss
the trail completely, spill drunken off the rocks,
and over stumps. Other times throw what they can

off the top, wait for the echoes to drop. I run
to see what's falling, like an angel
or dorm matron leading them to the gate.

The blond ones land in the garden.
So this is heaven: onions, carrots, garlic, peas,
planted and marked with string.

If I knew what to say, it would be simple.
You have fallen. It is all right.
But I say nothing and in the morning they are gone.

Widow's Song

1.

These days there is one crucifix between us. It fits in my palm:
a handgun, a quarter. Nothing happens when I hold it up to the light.

No turn of phrase, no metaphor, no look at us now. It does not ask
for better confessions. It says, *c'est la vie.* You run one hand over

the small mouth, the crosses we bear, the signs. I like to imagine the
blood – how quickly it runs to the piercings. Call it *sangre.* Call it
widow.

I want to die with my arms wide open, the way I let you tie me to the bed
and untie me to sleep side by side. As if we could stop it all with a nail

and a hammer, as if all we ever needed was another poem by me, a small
crucifix hanging on its nail above the phone in a nunnery by the sea.

2.

I said I would remember everything. The hands,
the size and shape, the moles, the heart lines.

I'd know the nails were bitten. Each scar's dissertation.
White skin under ring. What to say to friends at dinner

after the potatoes are passed, the rolls buttered,
the meat cut. I loved him and he died.

He died and I loved each trimmed hedge.
The smell of fresh-cut grass.

How often I walk there when I should sleep.
Lilac in June, always too strong for the house.

And the bed, when I think of him, smells of earth.
Too big for the room, his hands, what I see first.

Flip of pancake, paint that rail. Carry the child
back to bed. We lived in a house like this one.

Yesterday, I found a glove stuck in a snow bank.
Tore out each seam. Buried the needle in the yard.

           3.
I dreamt him again. The night – 1944,
in a shirt and a tie, flying a kite in front of St. Mary's.

He turned to me and asked for a dime, sometimes
if the world is a coin, let it rest in your palm.

Clutch it and the kite: I am
forty years old beside a man

in a rain coat. He holds out his hand
but I can't hear what he's saying.

As if there is glass between us, as if everything
I've ever turned to will break when I answer.

I am dreaming of a beautiful plate,
spinning at the top of a long pole

while I stand on his shoulders.
In my dream, he flies. All I want

is a hand but I am shy and reach instead
for a glass of water. The first time I saw him,

I knew.
He had such fine shoes.

4.
I left him by the river.
But I can't remember which river.
There are no bones left in my body.
Nothing inside me now to break.

I am so tired of the freak show,
widows drawing crooked to the trees,
stuffing the old shoes with leaves.
I wait beside some river without legs.

5.
It is my job to keep telling the stories no one else will tell.
Try to make sense out of them, rare flowers and I need lessons.

Lie down in the meadow and look. A dream goes like this:
light reaches the bed but I cannot remember making love,

fumble with absence, the table set with good china, knives
and two forks. Light the candles. Serve the fish.

Always too early to sleep. I've heard there is only
so much the living can share with the dead.

Who disagrees? We meet on the stairs and fifteen years
have passed. He formed the future in my mouth.

I am not surprised by what I do remember, what gifts
in a tongue promising, promising.

ASK FOR BIRDS

When I pray this evening I will ask for birds
White cranes circling the cliffs of my body.
           – Kelly Parsons

I will ask for birds, you said.
Said it calm, said it sure, made me blink.

I never know what to ask for.
Water? The blossom? The cave?

To give birth in a long, warm room?
Give me the roads, the fast curves with no shoulders.

Or the chair Grandfather built to watch
the morning rise its appointed rise above the glen.

You said the goose, the great guffaw
above the field. I want it, too.

And a body. I'd miss hair
down my back, in every trace of my mouth.

Or tea? I'll take it steaming
in a bright blue mug.

HEIRLOOMS

Grandmother Hills has hands
I'd like to remember.

She could wring a sheet dry
with one hand and iron it
with the other, bring her husband
breakfast in bed on a Sunday
after a night at the hotel
and when he refused to eat,
carry the tray back to the kitchen.

Who wouldn't smash the eggs on his face?

Trace these hands. Rub the knuckles.
Draw each finger down to the lifeline,
touch the heart, tender in the middle of the palm.

These hands have soothed a child drowned.
A child deaf. A child cold, beaten by the quiet
diseases of the poor. Neighbours come running
to look. Grandmother pregnant again!

So soon what we collect is carried to the curb:
twelve kids and the Depression, galoshes, ice box,
hat pins, three-legged chair. And what we keep,
who decides? With so many things to place behind
the glass, to dust, to savour and to bury, Grandmother,
thank you for these hands, these hands, these hands.

WAKE

Robins bring me to the porch,
to a clothesline pinned to the wall
where I see my mother's hands,
that same memory returning.

And without asking permission,
more birds come. I cannot
tell you their names
or speak of their migrations

when the sun stands straight above the house
and so many buds have to balance on the breeze
while cedars shake in the wake of all this wind.

I have told you what brought me here,
but I cannot explain why I linger, remembering
the least important things.

NOTHING SPECIAL

Two weeks before he dies, Grandfather
grips the wheel though the car's not moving.
Bends his head to suck the fag. The herons gawk
at the road, at the cars that could pass for fish
in this light. Patience offers little reprieve.

The country music and the fan are blasting,
making the temperature in his Chrysler
a summer in Croatia, the Dalmatian Coast
with Steph and Crava, smoking hand-rolled
and working their slow way through the docks.

Always waiting, she thinks, my grandfather.
Offers a ride whether she wants one or not.
Today there's a fire in the tunnel, cars stuck
like long tails on both sides of the slough.

But she is young, worse than young,
next week, she'll be sixteen.
Her days are days and nothing special.
Favourite supper: white and starch.

Her grandfather takes a quarter
from the coin tray as if his car's a slot machine
and all he has to do is test his luck.
It doesn't shine but he wants her
to keep it.

If she were older, she would save it,
would know what he meant:
Find a box with gold clasp,
black velvet lining. Spit at the thing
until it shines.

Rain

She's missing the rain, its drift of circles
languishing on the driveway.

She stares at the onions in the small garden,
the old bike against the gate — these are the threads —

she thinks, the frayed edges of another day gone, a day
she might have flown to Rome, walked the splendour

of the ancient worlds, twirled in full skirt under da Vinci's
soft elegies. But she is here: Clematis and the shiver

of their blooms, wind on bare arms, autumn light
so weak it leans against the house. Gets caught leaning.

THREE

BIG SKY

Room enough for bees.
For Mother's fat hands
and even fatter wrists.
Her pigs.

Room enough for sleeping.
The small beds, tidied, rowed.
The moon quiet and lazy
in its dreams.

Room enough for the broken-
hearted. For Max. For Belle.
You and Moonie. Renee's
loopy horse.

Room enough for contrition.
The first petal from
the daisy or the last.
These sweet confessions.

SYLVAN GLEN

I keep my children vaccinated
and registered with Child Find,
belted in the back seat of the Volvo,
bicycles tuned, helmets tied tight.
At the pool, drill the lifeguards,
make sure they keep their eyes open wide.

I never tell my children about the glen,
how each summer someone died
predictably in a snarl of sun, teenagers
double-daring the new ones to jump
off the bridge – which everybody did,
eventually – jumped to the river and the rocks below.

Nobody told us we'd live forever.
Our mothers swam upstream, smoked
by the parking lot, killed suckers with salt.
Thirty years later, the park's deserted,
but I don't tell my kids about the glen,
summers nobody knew how long they'd last.

BEDSIDE

At the side of his mother's bed,
my husband's a monument
about to be bronzed and cast
with the other men in the plaza,
the ones that look real but
break apart in your hands
if you touch them.

For hours he caresses
her arm, absent-mindedly
strokes the face, each pale cheek.
Raises a straw to lips. Straightens
the bangs with a baby's brush,
bows his head when he cries.

When he leaves the room
for a glass of water, she dies.
Finally, the room to herself.
No one mumbling. No one making sense.
Not one man folding ribbon,
tying a fresh, red bow in her hair.

Hide the Pies

Almost sixteen, Helen must go
to the deaf and dumb school,
in Belleville, travel with the doctor on the train.

Evelyn believes what they tell her – it's 1939,

no time for good decisions – *She'll speak*,
he whispers, points to a baby in a woman's dress,
little fingers curling the edges of the hem.

What can anyone give? Evelyn strokes
her daughter's cheek with one hand,
braids the soft hair with the other.

Might Helen learn to mime this world?
The smell of peeling apples, Harry and his
block of ice? Two peppermints in a back hip-pocket?

Helen loves sugar, puts as many fingers as she can
from mouth to bowl. They have to hide the pies.
Before anything gets decided, they play a game,

the world so much smaller if it's rhymed, all cakes
patted down, sweet in Helen's hands. Not this world
of men in overcoats or ties, a town called Belleville

where Helen dies two months into first term
while Evelyn dreams them both in a field
feeding horses next to the barn, apples, grass.

Pneumonia, they pronounce, *water on the lungs*.
Our Helen, fingers they have rubbed clean,
fingers kissed with sugar.

THE MYRIAD SYMPATHIES

Show me how to live after something like this.
It makes me so mad the way McDonalds continues
to serve a billion hamburgers while under the ground

in the silver coffin we picked out lies Mother
in her lavender dress, opal earrings, and hands
folded over some stranger's plastic rosary.

And the root beer at A & W still tastes the same
served in the frosted glasses they keep ready in the freezer
while my father sleeps on the couch. I'm so mad

we had pork chops and scalloped potatoes for dinner last night
and then watched *Jeopardy* and *The Wheel of Fortune*
followed by *The Weather Network* because

we wanted to know when it might stop.
I washed and dried the dishes, borrowed
my father's boots and walked a half-hour

one way and a half-hour back so I wouldn't get lost
in the storm while a man died on the highway
but they didn't release his name

like it was captured somewhere inside
the mouths of the morning commuters,
Jesus, what was that guy doing?

And how does anything get done
when four out of five of us are attending funerals?
I can't suck another mint, peel an apple,

jog on the spot or brush my teeth.
I refuse to open one more Hallmark card, refuse to eat
one more bite of Aunt Meg's shepherd's pie.

These are the small defiances I can claim.

I watch my father sleep. His teeth sit in a glass
on the coffee table. Without them his cheeks change
from Dad to Old Man in an instant.

49

Taxidermist

A robin lies on its side
on the front step. Our rooms
too small for the dead,

but mother says
she'll live on in the stories
we'll tell. So sure of this,
she never stops talking.

Think Paul, from high school,
basement full of birds and
taxidermy guides, jars
of shocked obsidian eyes.

What would I do with
so many birds?

Mother crochets by candlelight.
If she pricks her finger,
maybe she will sleep.
Shuffles to the cemetery
in her robe and slippers.

Think of cats. There are so many.
Place the robin under the tree,
shut the door behind me.

LULLABY

My mother's hands are small
like the first star above the house.
The star I wished on as a child.
Still wish on. Sometimes,

when I hear a train whistle
whether I'm bent over the mower
or heading for the car, I am sure
she'll be home for supper.

It is a small star
but the first to break
the darkening sky
of childhood:

eyes squished shut,
fingers crossed, ready
to make a wish: so easy,
an inexperienced heart.

STILL LIFE

A green stool.
Two pillows.

The only light, one circle
over a corner of a chair.

Father, in his uniform,
lumps the wooden floor
with hulky snores, and blocks
the doorway to the kitchen.

The daughter steps closer,
bends to feel his breath
on her cheek, bristles
at the dark heat on the fingers.

She squats, squints.
Checks his pockets
for change.

It could be a small animal
she is greeting, darkness
this feral dream.

Her hand
rising like a fist
full of coins,
grubby moons
upon his shoulder.

GRIEF IN THE WORLD

December. Traffic's bad.
Nobody's moving. Moon squats
on Mill Hill. I want witnesses.
Want to climb the Calypso Trail
in one giant leap and kiss the moon
on the mouth. Wrap my arms
around it, say, *How did you know?*

STROKE

When I think of him blind and scared
he'd never speak again, I am certain I have never known suffering.
Never known cruelty or absence, either, never the weight of them:
his arms dopey rags, his fingers slow, who to dial for help,
the wife out, *don't know where*, the seeing-eye dog
and its four white paws witnessing the unthinkable
writhing of the master on the kitchen floor.

When I think of standing beside his bed in the hall
in Emergency, gowned and labelled, lips a pale distance
from the heart, I piece together the story: a helicopter
whirring over the strait, taking him from floor to cot to hospital
queue, the awful noise and the awful silence, the way we had to

lean into him to get out of a great and unidentified wind,
then lean into ourselves. We leave him there,
our brother, behind a curtain he could not see
but sensed was a brand new room, beside
the invisible, the arterial blood, waiting. And

I think of the heron at the pond last summer, the thin
blue line of bird at the edge, the gift of goldfish swimming
under the pale light, sky a mere branch, the heron
waiting like he had all the time in the world and could
strike or not strike at the stone, the spaces between stones.

HER BREATHING, FOR EXAMPLE

He is sixteen when he sees his mother, with the man from Crawford Bay,
sitting by the window in the kitchen, laughing. Her hand touching the
throat as the stranger strikes a match and leads it to her cigarette; the boy

doesn't know what his father would do if he could walk through that door,
long home from war, lunch pail in his left hand, small bit of egg frying in
the pan on the stove; the stove she hated in the house she hated

and everybody knowing why it was built in such a hurry. But his father will
not walk in, not now, not ever. The boy glances at the green chair in the
living room, the heart having to shrink for a boy
to keep it in his chest.

He thinks of his future, thinks of her future: His mother will die
in a hospital bed and he will be led to her room by a dog. The dog will take
him to the chair beside her while she sleeps and he'll recall this day: the
man,

his mother, the kind of boy he was. He'll recall what he'd really wanted in
that kitchen in the small house above the lake in Nelson. What he really
wanted: a piano in the living room, pupils on hard chairs in the hall

outside a closed door, sure they were waiting for something good. Stepping
into rooms they'd never seen before, running water— not lugging buckets
from a well— dishes, and tablecloths and candlesticks, things

for small hands to take and turn into music. As his mother sleeps in that
hospital bed, he will pull the chair closer, and listen, the way he has heard
some blind men do, listen not to the story, not for the words; he'll listen to

her breathing, for example, the scratch of white shirt and tie, the sound a
hand makes on another hand. And in the darkness, he will put his head
close to but not on her chest, the heart, he's certain now, unable to hold
them, both.

FOUR

PRAISE FOR HUMANS

Some days she refuses to pray.
Refuses to tie up her shoes, wash the dishes, clean the ashtray.
Puts on her roller skates and turns the town into one fenced rink.
Twirl. Thatta' girl.

Her father's a fool. And the priest, too.
The war, positively. Koot Smith, definitely.
It ain't over til it's over? Tell someone who cares.
Downhill. Toe back.

She's dropped a dozen petals in the fountain.
Yesterday, found a four-leaf near the manse.
Anybody can whistle for a beer. Cute figure, too.
With legs like these, who needs wings?

Step on a crack and . . . She won't know.
Kiss a boy, why bother? She could
flatten them. Bunch of noodles! Beans for brains.
Hail Mary, full of grace . . . knocked up, yuk!

Pray to a pregnant woman full of God. No way.
Kneel in the fields until they're empty. Penny a bushel.
Nickel an hour. Don't cry. There's a song coming,
she'll keep her ear on the rail. Sense? Worth its weight, I guess.

Air Travel

Swallows dip and glide and almost run into things
because the sky's a cheap bar, the patrons drunk
on spring and having babies. These are the birds
he waits for. Soundless gliders, never looking behind
them, never two left feet. They build nests in the carport,
mud shacks in the eaves. With the sun pushing lilac to bloom,
they arrive, the end of their tails pale heralds of spring
and all its longings. He wants to know. Tell him.
Tell him how to love this way. Which season.
And, tell him, he must not wait. We are birds.
We will never leave a trail in the snow.

STONES

In this house we sing folk songs of
planting onions on our graves so
visitors are sure to shed a tear, pick
handfuls of green stems with heads bowed,
eyes lowered, dreaming of salad with dinner.

We think it's pretty funny, the one
about the girl committing suicide,
Little cross-eyed girl upon the hill. Mom
teaching us to laugh at everything: broken
bunnies on sale at Stedman's, cancer, polio,
blind dogs. When *she* dies, it's not so funny.

We consider buying onions at Loblaw's.
Tune the guitars and practice singing off key.
But when I hear she wants a flat stone,
a child's stone, to mark her grave
I refuse, stamp my feet, charge the executor
with low comedy: this is serious, my mother is dead!

Who can accept a name flat in the grass?
No capitals, no curlicues beside the brothers
and sisters who died so young,
their level markers matching
the small years lived by the lake.
She's a grown woman, not a clown.

When I'm passing by, I'll snatch them up and cry . . .
quit horsing around! I want pink granite, an angel
trumpeting her way to heaven, not my mother, flat
on her back, beside the lilies, beside the onions, beside the stones.

GROUND

A small garden. One bench
beside a thin bamboo. There's
room for you to stretch out
the bad leg, take a big, long drag
from one of your Menthols
and let the smoke rise to the tip
of something still in bloom.

Forgiveness, calm in the eyries.

I am burying your ashes, Dad.
Digging them into the soil
with two hands, touching all
of you this time, elbow, chin,
forgive me, cock, ankle,
sorry, hip, ass, tongue,
forehead, bone, watch
you slowly settle in.
Watch the rocks, the slugs,
the roots make new rooms.

THE SHALLOW POOL

The families fish Chapala's waters, sell the catch
at makeshift market stalls. Hands mend nets,
wrap fish, as if they are speaking in sign, hands

opening and closing as her life returns in waves. The lake
so still after the girl's death, no one can believe the water
that wooed her.

For weeks the fish float belly up to shore,
sorrow rushes to the shallow pools, silence,
a language for the drowned.

And at the funeral tongues bloat in the sun,
flounder on the rafts of rosaries as young priests
sniff out the edges of the sea. What little is spoken

trickles into an ear, the cup a hand might make
for an injured bird. One palm warming a butterfly
asleep. Another walking an insect to an open window.

WOODEN CHAIR

Never questions itself.
Never doubts.

Could not define the word
quibble. So easily
turns the other cheek.

Mother's the one who runs
her hands over the spindles

wonders
will it hold
will it hold.

DETAILS

I never noticed the dirt, couldn't tell you if they covered the mounds between funerals in cheap plastic so the men (whoever they were) could slip into the Legion across the street and buy a draft or two with a ham sandwich for lunch and then while they smoked a cigarette, answer the same questions they always answer: Who was it today and how did it go?

I never noticed how long it took us to drive from the church to the cemetery after the mass or how long my brother cried when the undertaker explained the importance of cement liners and how much they cost. He couldn't stop the tears or the moan that came with them like a cat we can't find in the alley, that small room, hot in the basement of Allison's Funeral Home, Hope Street.

I can tell you that we expected Bob to be the one to cry for us. He always cried and we let him cry, as if there was something wrong with him and not with us. We had to pick out the coffin because the burial was set for Tuesday. By the time we arrived at the cemetery, it was raining. The coffin already in the ground, tucked neatly in cement. The priest, far from his home in the Philippines, looked comfortable.

The brown skin, the robes, the accent, the prayers, new to us. I wanted to push him into the grave with my mother so he could tell us what it was really going to be like. But my brother who was still crying pointed to the priest's shoes and whispered, they're the kind of shoes he would wear if he were a priest, blunt not pointy, a wide and comfortable shoe made for walking the small villages among the orphans.

The Cormorant

Wings held by bone, the cormorant at low tide dries
in the lambent shore
and so

explains
the history of pathos:
two bedraggled wings, one oh-so-generous anchor.

MAKING JAM

When the phone rings, I stop making jam.
Remember the country, picking berries
through the last days of June, crouching
low to spot the ripe ones, our backs aching
with the strain, each long row, dizzy.
When the phone rings, I stop making jam.
My fingers sticky, can't use them to count
the seconds between *How is she?* and *Hello.*
Such a useless tongue.

In the pause, return to the field.
Hat and sundress, basket full of fruit.
I knock the jam off the counter:
the body's way of catching up
to bad news, makes a mess of the stove.
So much to clean in a kitchen.
The telephone sticky sweet.
The floor. I lick my fingers first,
one by one, an animal
licking her grief.

Humbly

I miss her most right now,
after dinner, the dishes done,
when I am tired of the refrigerator,
the marvelous silence, the irritable hum,
her apron folded over in the sun.

HOPE

I know that hope is the hardest love we carry.
— Jane Hirshfield, *The Lives of the Heart*

Ask my mother to sing. Only her voice, these days,
consoles me. She sings of buttons and bows,
apples and trains, men as far away as the moon.
Her world during the war, the whole town to herself.

But she's no dreamer. She never dreams.
She dries dishes while she sings,
folds a dead baby's socks, irons the aprons
for the factory.

Her songs have been passed
from slave to tramp to radio,
because she says all the good hymns
are passed through somebody's heart.

She misses the mass in Latin though,
as if the strange tongues were really angels
speaking about ordinary things: Some days,
she can't answer me at all.

Everything freezes to that *otherworld*:
the brothers and the sisters gone to war,
a mute upstairs, another sister lame,
her mother on her knees, not praying,

scrubbing, so you can eat off her floors,
onion pie cut in four, smelt, pan-fried,
thick with the memory of butter,
any rooms but these.

THE CRAZY MAPS

Mother dies in a hospital bed in Peterborough,
thirty miles north of where she was born.

The leaves turn and fall into snow, roads slippery tonight,
a storm of memory in the headlights and this one bullies

its way to centre stage. The truth: she's gone.
It's snowing. We can't find Father.

When he hears the news, he drives in circles,
lost in the cul-de-sacs south of the city, amazed

how streets he'd driven all his life narrow and disappear.
In his red car, window cracked an inch, smoke fumes

a thin line toward starlight. Cigarette after cigarette
dropped in the suburbs on the crazy maps of grief.

A stranger, arriving after midnight, can't say
where he's been, coat open, tie askew,

everybody thinking he was the one who would go first.
Silence replaces her and snow spins a requiem

outside the window with city lights fading
under full cloud, the first hours without her.

This early fall morning, October, no one speaks
of the future or of the past. We are stuck

in private thoughts, the swirl and pull of the season,
sounds we hear when we sleep, furnace, fridge, fact.

Surely, we had a hand in it. Surely, had we known
some other way to love, she would have made it home.

Acknowledgements

The poem, "The crazy maps", won *Arc Magazine's* Poem of the Year Contest. "Her breathing, for example" won the Rona Murray Poetry Prize and "The myriad sympathies" received an honourable mention in the 2004 Bliss Carmen Poetry Contest. "Love poem" is published in *String to Bow*, the chapbook of winning love poems from the "Looking for Love Poems" contest by Leaf Press.

I would like to thank the Canada Council and the B.C. Arts Council for providing some of the time to write these poems. My thanks also to the editors of the literary magazines where many of the poems have been published: *Arc, The Malahat Review, Prairie Fire, Prairie Journal, The Bellingham Review, Quills, Fiddlehead, The New Quarterly,* and *sub Terrain.* Other poems were published in the chapbooks, *Briefly Perfect* and *Masks,* edited by Patrick Lane.

Billie Stenson's my first, my last, my in-between reader. Lucky me. Thanks, Billie. Marlene Cookshaw read and edited an early draft of the manuscript from a room on the top floor of her home on Pender Island where all fine editors live. Thank you, Marlene. And finally, enormous gratitude to Wendy Morton and the poets at *Planet Earth* for making all things poetic!